Boyd Norton's

PhotoJournal

Voyageur Press

Copyright © 1990 by Boyd Norton

All rights reserved. No part of this work may be reproduced or used in any form by any means—graphic, electronic, or mechanical, including photocopying, recording, taping, or any information storage and retrieval system—without written permission of the publisher.

Printed in Hong Kong
90 91 92 93 94 5 4 3 2 1

Library of Congress Cataloging-in-Publication Data

Norton, Boyd.
Boyd Norton's photojournal / Boyd Norton.
p. cm.
ISBN 0-89658-126-8
1. Nature photography—Handbooks, manuals, etc.
TR721.N66 1990
778.9'3—dc20
90-30864
CIP

Published by Voyageur Press, Inc.
P.O. Box 338, 123 North Second Street
Stillwater, MN 55082 U.S.A.
In Minn 612-430-2210
Toll-free 800-888-9653

Distributed in Canada by Whitecap Books
Vancouver/Toronto

Voyageur Press books are also available at discounts for quantities for educational, fundraising, premium, or sales-promotion use. For details contact the marketing manager. Please write or call for our free catalog of publications.

To Barbara. Thanks for sharing it all with me.

Contents

On Photography ***7***

Photographer's Personal Note Pages ***12***
Plus Informative Captions

Exposure Tips ***112***

Double and Multiple Exposures ***113***

Reciprocity Failure in Color Films ***114***

Cold Weather Photography ***116***

Nighttime/Low Light Photography ***117***

Shooting the Moon ***118***

Names and Addresses ***119***

Photographer's Personal Directory ***124***

Using the Gray Card ***128***

Her name is Teddy. She's an Alaskan brown bear, or grizzly, *Ursus arctos*. Her home is the McNeil Rive Sanctuary. For several years I've been photographing her and we've become friends. The cub show here is now grown. And recently Teddy showed me her two new cubs *from only fifteen feet away.* Amazin friendliness for an animal with such a ferocious reputation. While grizzlies elsewhere aren't doing well as species, Teddy and friends at McNeil still roam wild and free and protected. Hang in there Teddy, we nee you. Lens: Leica 560mm. Film: Fujichrome 50.

A Note on the Captions

Within the limitations of the space on each page, I've tried to make the photo captions convey important information about *how* the photographs were made and, in some instances, *why*. In most of the captions, I haven't included such information as f-stop and shutter speed because it is simply not important. But in a few cases where it is significant in understanding an effect, I have included f-stop and shutter speed data, for example, slow shutter speed to blur motion, a small f-stop to maximize depth of field.

In the same vein, I haven't mentioned the kind of camera used. For the most part, I use Leicas, but it really doesn't matter whether the picture was made with a Leica R4sp or a Leica R5 or R6. I have included, however, the lens focal length information because different lenses create different perspectives, and lens choice is an important factor in rendering scenes and subjects in certain ways.

)n the cover:

t looks like a laugh, but it's a yawn. These juvenile cheetahs in Maasai Mara Game Reserve in Kenya vere waiting for Mom to lead them off on the evening's hunt. They had been napping most of the fternoon, but I waited around until they awakened. With wildlife photography, you have to be patient—nd ready. You never know what to expect. They started grooming each other and suddenly one of them roke into this big yawn. Lens: Leica 280mm APO-Telyt. Film: Kodachrome 200.

)n page one:

Timing and patience are key elements in good wildlife photography. This lion in Tanzania's Serengeti National Park had been sleeping soundly and showed no signs of stirring. But I waited anyway and finally got him yawning grandly. Lens: Leica 400mm. Film: Kodachrome 64.

)n page two:

A tripod is essential for most good closeup photography. With the camera on a stable platform, you can stop the lens down for good depth of field for pictures with a crisp edge of sharpness. Soft light from an overcast sky helps bring out subtle color of these tundra dogwood blossoms on Alaska's Kenai Peninsula. Lens: Leica 100mm macro. Film: Kodachrome 200.

Not all photography has to be realistic. I love to experiment with impressionistic interpretations (ordinary things. This brush stroke rendering of yellow flowers was done by making sixteen exposures o a single frame. Your camera must have multiple exposure capability. Use a motor drive and hold th multiexposure lever or button in while shooting and counting off the exposures. Here's the formula to ge the correct exposure: For sixteen exposures and ISO 64 film, set your camera's exposure setting to IS(1000 and take a normal reading. (Don't forget to reset to normal speed when you're done!) Lens: Leic 100mm macro. Film: Kodachrome 64.

On Photography

I can look at a fine photograph and sometimes I can hear music. —Ansel Adams

Photography. For many of us it's not just a pleasure but a passion, a passion for capturing the beauty of the world around us. And that world is full of visual richness. But it's also full of visual chaos, and it is our job as photographers to create order out of that chaos. Not an easy task sometimes.

Photography has been called the art of seeing, and it's true. We need to look beyond the superficial and really begin to see things. In a way, it's a little like bringing back the wonders of childhood. Remember how, when you were a youngster, everything was new and exciting? A whole world of visual richness awaited your discovery. It's still there. But as adults we've lost that childlike sense of wonder. When you take time to look and observe carefully, you'll find that very ordinary things can become extraordinary photographic subjects.

What things? The possibilities are limited only by your imagination and ability to perceive. Colors, shapes, forms, lines, textures, and patterns of ordinary things are often visually exciting—and challenging to capture on film. You don't need to travel to exotic lands to find beauty. Take a careful look at the things you pass by every day around the house or on the way to work. Like signs. Or fences. Or ornate doors and windows. How about shadows or grass or foliage or the sky?

To become a better photographer, you should photograph as often as possible. Don't just take the camera out on special occasions or trips. Make your camera a part of everyday life. Give yourself assignments. Pretend that a magazine has asked you to document your town or job or friends or lifestyle or environment. Sometimes it is helpful to pick a theme to photograph. You could choose water. Or the different kinds of trees near your home. Or common objects found in your kitchen. And if you really want to challenge yourself, choose something a little more abstract: the wind, or sound, or fear. Here's something that's fun and challenging: Take a ten-foot piece of string and stake out a territory somewhere using that string. Then, within that ten-foot radius, shoot a

Here's a great technique for making photographs with a heightened impression of speed or movement, a in this shot of running wildebeest in Tanzania's Serengeti National Park. The technique is called a blur-pan Use a 300mm or 400mm lens with a shutter speed of 1/15 second. Follow the moving animals as thoug you were panning with a video or motion picture camera. Use a motor drive and try to time your pan t the speed of the moving object. And shoot lots because you're never sure what you'll get. Lens: Leic 400mm. Film: Kodachrome 64.

whole roll of film. I guarantee that you will begin to look closely at things you hadn't looked at before.

★ ★ ★

The word photography is derived from two Greek words: *photos,* meaning *light,* and *graphos,* meaning *to write.* Light is the essence of photography, and to become good writers of light, we must become masters of light. The two attributes of light we must understand and control are *quantity* and *quality.*

In photography, exposure has to do with the quantity of light. The most exciting, visually dynamic scene will fail to become a good picture if the exposure is awry. Fortunately, modern cameras have excellent light metering systems that can be depended upon to yield proper exposure in most situations. Still, there are times when the meter is fooled into giving exposures that are wrong for the scene or the subject. Very light or very dark subjects or subjects that have strong backlighting create problems. Learn to understand your camera's metering system. Elsewhere in this notebook are discussions on exposure tips and instructions on using a gray card. And when you encounter tricky lighting situations, take notes on the exposures you use (that's what this notebook is for!). Learn from your mistakes—and successes.

Quality of light is another matter. It's more subjective. No meter will give you a measure of the quality, which is something you learn to gauge by experience. Quality of light has to do with the mood or feeling of a picture. A scene photographed in midday sunlight will have a harsh quality. The same scene in overcast lighting will be softer, quieter.

Undoubtedly you've already noticed how the quality of light changes with the time of day. Early morning or late afternoon sunlight has a warmth that creates a certain feeling in pictures, tending to be a bit softer. And, because the light's source is at a low angle in the sky, nearly horizontal, early morning or late afternoon sunlight helps to bring out texture, and the long shadows created give a depth and dimension to landscapes.

Bright sunlight in the middle of the day is one of the worst kinds of

It's easy to get good lightning shots at night. Set your camera on a tripod, select B (for "Bulb") on th
shutter speed dial, and hold the shutter open with a locking cable release. I hold a black card over the fror
of the lens and remove it when I think enough time has passed for the next strike, and then I put it back
I'm trying for several lightning bolts in the same picture. In this case, I recorded two separate strikes
Lens: Nikkor 35-135 zoom at maximum aperture (f/3.5). Film: Kodachrome 64.

lighting for many things. It's harsh. It's very contrasty. Most films simply can't handle the extremes of contrast. Shadows become black with no detail. And highlights wash out—again with no detail. Landscapes look flat, and often there is haze created by ground heating. Midday is a good time to be taking a nap under a tree rather than photographing.

Overcast light has a wonderful quality. For photographing people or flowers it's great. Subtle color is rendered beautifully, with good distinctions between hues and tones. As you look through the photographs in this book, you'll note that many of them were made under such conditions—overcast skies—and, in some cases, even stormy weather. So, when the weather turns bad, don't put your camera away. Keep shooting.

★ ★ ★

Photography is the popular art form of our culture. We buy more than 15 million cameras a year and shoot almost 13 *billion* pictures. With those kinds of numbers, it might almost seem as though all the great pictures have been made. But of course, they haven't. In this beautiful world we live in, there's an infinite variety of photographic interpretation. Each time I put the camera to my eye, I'm entering a new world for the first time. That's the excitement of it. And the challenge.

Enjoy!

—Boyd Norton

Too many people put their cameras away when the weather turns bad. To me it's a great time t photograph because the soft light of overcast skies helps to bring out subtle color in many subjects. Th pattern of autumn foliage in New Hampshire's White Mountain National Forest was aided greatly by th overcast sky. Lens: Leica 180mm. Film: Kodachrome 64.

Notes

This magnificent bull elephant in Tanzania's Ngorongoro Crater made a few threatening gestures a
though he were going to charge—not a pleasant prospect, even in a safari vehicle. But he settled down t
graze and pose nicely. Sadly, elephants may be threatened with extinction unless we all support
worldwide ban on ivory. Lens: Leica 180mm. Film: Kodachrome 200.

Notes

There's an old photojournalistic adage about how to get a great shot: F/8 and *be there!* This is a case being there. I was up before dawn to prepare for this picture of Alaska's Augustine Volcano from Chen Head in Kamishak Bay. It was three months after a major eruption. Before the sun came over the horizo it illuminated the sky with this lovely glowing color—a perfect background for the steaming volcano. Len Leica 70-210mm zoom. Film: Kodachrome 64.

Notes

Exercise some care and judgment when determining exposure for ice and snow, or anything else that i light and bright. Remember, the meter tries to make all that white an 18 percent gray, and therefore th picture will be too dark, or underexposed. Try to meter off something close to a middle or 18 percen gray, or use the gray card in this notebook (check the instructions first). This scene is of Portage Glacie in Alaska. Lens: Leica 70-210mm zoom. Film: Kodachrome 64.

Notes

It ain't easy rolling out of a warm sleeping bag on a frosty morning at 11,000 feet in the Rockies. But it's definitely worth it photographically. I found this frost-nipped globeflower and leaves just before the sun came up. The predawn light helped to convey a sense of coldness. The camera was, of course, on a tripod. Lens: Leica 100mm macro. Film: Fujichrome 100.

Notes

Photographing sunrises and sunsets can sometimes be a little tricky. The key is *not* to underexpose. If you make your exposure with the sun occupying a part of the picture you will underexpose it and lose color and detail. I always meter off the sky to the right or the left of the sun, far enough away so that the sun isn't in the picture. Using that as a basic exposure, I then recompose the picture with the sun placed where I want it. It's always smart to bracket exposures as well. Locale: Kenya's Maasai Mara Game Reserve. Lens: Leica 560mm. Film: Kodachrome 64.

Notes

A low angle or side lighting helps to bring out texture in things. Late-afternoon low-angle sun emphasize the ripple patterns in these dunes near Yei Bechei in Arizona's Monument Valley. I used an ultra-wide angle lens very close to the ground to give emphasis to the ripples. Stopping down to f/22 gave me dept of field sufficient to keep everything sharp from foreground to background. Lens: Leica 21mm. Film Kodachrome 64.

Notes

The mountain gorillas of Rwanda and Zaire are such magnificent animals, so gentle and tolerant. But this is some of the toughest photography I've ever done because of the habitat: high altitude rain forest. And they don't call it rain forest for nothing. The combination of overcast skies and thick forest make for very dim lighting. Kodachrome 200 is the film of choice here. Even then, I was forced on occasion to use a slow shutter speed: 1/30 second. I had to brace the camera against a tree where possible. And I squeezed the shutter release sloooowly to avoid camera shake. Lens: Leica 70-210mm zoom.

Notes

The bird life in Africa is astounding in its quality and color. This is a superb starling in Kenya's Tsa National Park. I had noted that this particular bird seemed to have a favorite perch on the branch of acacia tree. So I set up the camera with a Leica 400mm Telyt lens and waited. By shooting at maximu aperture, I was able to throw the background totally out of focus and keep it undistracting. Fil Kodachrome 200.

Notes

Quality of light is so important. I waited until the afternoon sun was near setting to photograph tl cheetah in Maasai Mara Game Reserve in Kenya. The light was softened by thin clouds on the horizc and the warmth of the light emphasized the beauty of the cheetah's fur. Lens: Leica APO 280mm. Fil Kodachrome 200.

Notes

What's the best lens for photographing grizzly bears? *The longest telephoto you can get!* Actually, thes bears at McNeil River State Game Sanctuary in Alaska are quite tolerant of people. I've had them wande as close as fifteen feet from me and they've never acted aggressively. This shot is another example crucial timing in good wildlife shots. Ms. Mouse and her three cubs had been fishing when another bea approached. I caught this pose as they looked anxiously at the newly arrived bear. Lens: Leica 560mm Film: Kodachrome 200.

Notes

Bali is a photographer's dream. Everywhere you turn are rich colors and wonderful lines and shapes ar patterns. I was struck by the lovely pattern formed by these lines of terraced rice paddies near Besakih. used the maximum focal length of 210mm on my Leica 70-210mm zoom to isolate the pattern. I also use a polarizing filter to eliminate glare and bring out the rich color. Film: Kodachrome 64.

Notes

With all of the grand scenery in Alaska, it's sometimes easy to overlook the details. Yet it's often the sm things that give a distinct character to a place. Tundra is a common feature of the Alaska landscap Because of a severe climate, tundra plants are often minute—sometimes an inch or so high. On the tund of Lake Clark National Park I found this lovely combination of ferns and bog cranberries. Shooting or tripod for the sharpest image, I used a Leica 100mm macro lens. Film: Kodachrome 64.

Notes

Aesthetics are an integral part of the culture of Bali. Everywhere you turn there are carvings, statue and paintings, all expressions of beauty important to the Balinese. The statue was sitting by the edge o rice paddy. Someone had taken time to place a hibiscus flower behind the ear. The contrasts betwe muted gray and brilliant red and between hard stone and soft blossom are what attracted me to this sh Lens: Leica 35-70mm zoom. Film: Kodachrome 64.

Notes

This is a constructed image. Both parts of the image, the sun and the cheetah, were photographed Tanzania's Serengeti National Park a few hours apart. I wish I had been able to get the sunset to coincic with the cheetah climbing the rock outcrop, but it didn't happen. So I combined them later by sandwichir the slides together and making a high resolution duplicate of the composite. Lens for the cheetah: Lei 400mm Telyt. Lens for the sunset: Leica 560mm Telyt. Film for both: Kodachrome 64.

Notes

When you start getting bored with terrestrial photography, look up! The sky itself can be a fascinati subject, with the ever-changing patterns of clouds and storms and colors. I call them skyscapes as o posed to landscapes. I photographed these wispy cirrus clouds while on magazine assignment in Hamb Provincial Park in British Columbia. A polarizing filter darkened the sky to heighten the contrast betwe the clouds and sky. Lens: Leica 70-210mm. Film: Kodachrome 64.

Notes

I've never understood why Africa was called the Dark Continent. To me it's a place of light and brightnes and life. I've never found another place that has the incredible sunrises and sunsets that you find in Eas Africa. There's something about the atmosphere, perhaps dust in the air, that gives color like I've neve seen elsewhere. This sunset in Tanzania's Serengeti National Park was made with a Leica 400mm Tely with a 2X extender, giving 800mm focal length. Film: Kodachrome 64.

Notes

In Arizona's Monument Valley there are a few places where water collects after a rare rainfall. I found th pool in the middle of the day when the sun was high and harsh, so I planned my return here for lat afternoon. The setting sun provided a warm glow of color to enhance the already colorful sandstone Mitten Butte. Lens: Leica 70-210mm. Film: Fujichrome 50.

Notes

Lake Marie is almost 11,000 feet in elevation in the Snowy Range of Wyoming. On this morning, ther were some very thin clouds on the horizon as the sun came up, and they had the effect of a diffusion filte softening the light and muting the color. The effect reinforced the tranquility of the place. I used a 21m ultra-wide-angle lens, lying on my stomach at the edge of the lake. Stopped down to f/22, there w enough depth of field to keep both the foreground rocks and the background mountain sharp. Film Fujichrome 100.

Notes

Scant rain falls in the desert country of Utah. And when it does, it dries quickly. There are a few sma streams in Arches National Park, fed by springs, but in the blistering heat of summer they dry up. Th shot of dried mud was made in Courthouse Wash and it was the subtle color and texture of this scene th appealed to me. It's an austere land, but those dried cottonwood leaves show that it's not devoid of lif Lens: Leica 100mm macro. Film: Kodachrome 64.

Notes

French Impressionist? No, just a reflection in a pond at Home Ranch in Colorado. One of the gr qualities of water is the way it takes light and images and reflects and transforms them. Nothing magi about it. But you do have to spend time looking and observing. Of course, a perfectly still pond create perfect image. The key is to wait until there are subtle ripples or disturbances that alter the reality. E your heart out, Monet. Lens: Leica 70-210mm zoom. Film: Kodachrome 64.

Notes

The Elk River Valley in northern Colorado. I liked the look of starkness and cleanness of this aspen tre
and to make all those austere lines stand out boldly, I positioned myself so that the tree was backlit again
a dark background of spruce trees. Metering was the tough part. If I let the meter be influenced by th
dark background, the tree would have been *over*exposed. Metering off the white tree would have cause
*under*exposure, so I used some medium-toned ground cover in the foreground for my reading. Len
Leica 400mm Telyt. Film: Kodachrome 64.

Notes

The slickrock and canyon country of Utah is among my favorite places in the world. Most years this deser explodes in colorful flowers in May or June. These vivid claret cup cactus blossoms were found in Arche National Park. Bright sunlight would have been too harsh and contrasty for this scene, so I waited fo some cloud cover to soften the light. A tripod was essential to hold the camera steady and give the cris sharpness this picture demands. Lens: Leica 100mm macro. Film: Kodachrome 64.

Notes

Because rainbows are so ethereal, you need to be especially careful with exposure. When in doubt, it's best to underexpose. Overexposure—even by a small amount—will wash out the delicate colors. Incidentally, you can often intensify the color of a rainbow by using a polarizing filter. But note, as you rotate it, there's one position where the rainbow will disappear entirely! This one occurred after a thunderstorm in Wyoming's Snowy Range. Lens: Leica 70-210mm zoom. Film: Kodachrome 64.

Notes

These layers of overlapping ferns made for a nice pattern composition. The intense green symbolizes the lushness of the coastal rain forest of Alaska here in a Sitka spruce forest along the shore of Kachemak Bay on the Kenai Peninsula. This is the kind of shot that dictates the use of a tripod. The stable platform allows a slow shutter speed and a small aperture for good depth of field. Lens: Leica 100mm macro. Film: Fujichrome 100.

Notes

During an Alaskan summertime you can have long days of photography. This shot was made near midnigh in the Wrangell-St. Elias National Preserve. Mt. Sanford, 16,237 feet, glowed like a jewel near the tundra lake that I had flown to by bush plane. The best exposure, I found, was obtained by metering from the blue sky to the side of the mountain. Lens: Leica 100mm macro. Film: Kodachrome 64.

Notes

Sometimes the most visually exciting things are trampled underfoot. What can be more common—and s often overlooked—than grass? When you get down to ground level you'll discover a whole world a beaut Try it sometime: Put a 105mm or a 180mm lens on an extension tube and crawl around exploring the low plants. Shoot wide open so there's very shallow depth of field—too much depth of field creates visu clutter in foregrounds and backgrounds. Lens: Leica 180mm. Film: Fujichrome 100.

Notes

I couldn't believe it. I was tooling along a backroad in eastern Utah near the Colorado River and fou some old abandoned buildings on which some artist had painted wonderful murals. So I slammed on t brakes and piled out with the camera. I love the surreal aspect of this scene: A doorway to another wor Lens: Leica 100mm macro. Film: Fujichrome 50.

Notes

This is the business end of a black rhino in Ngorongoro Crater in Tanzania. Fortunately, he was mo interested in grazing than in charging. Sadly, these magnificent animals are threatened with extincti because of poaching. Contributions to World Wildlife Fund and African Wildlife Foundation (addresses the end of this notebook) can help preserve the rhino and elephants in Africa. Lens: Leica 560mm Tely Film: Kodachrome 200.

Notes

A snow and ice-covered log along a stream in Colorado's Mr. Zirkel Wilderness Area represents anotl of those wonderful attributes of water. Exposure was tricky on this: All that brightness caused the me to underexpose too much. So I took my meter reading off a nice gray-colored rock nearby and based exposure on that. I needed a fairly small aperture (f/11) to give enough depth of field to keep the log a rocks sharp, and the resultant slow shutter speed (1/4 second) blurred the water nicely. Lens: Leica 210mm zoom. Film: Kodachrome 64.

Notes

The Sepilok Orangutan Sanctuary in Borneo is an enchanting place, but because of the rain forest settin
it's often overcast. And with active young orangutans running around and playing, you need a high spe
film for an action-stopping shutter speed and reasonable depth of field. My film of choice for the
conditions is Kodachrome 200 for its crisp sharpness and great color. Lens: Leica 70-210mm zoom.

Notes

Storms and clouds add drama to landscapes, especially when fired by the color of sunrise or sunset. It ha been clear all afternoon and I didn't expect much sunset color here on a boat trip in Kenai Fjords Natior Park in Alaska. But as we dropped anchor for the night, some clouds rolled in and added a perfect touch the scene. Those silhouetted trees give a nice balance to the composition. Lens: Leica 100mm macr Film: Kodachrome 64.

Notes

These fallen leaves covered by the slush of a puddle in the forest signify the end of fall and the beginning o
winter. It's easy to overlook details like these. When wandering around looking for photographic subjects
examine your surroundings carefully, especially things on the ground. The overcast light dictated a slo
shutter speed (1/4 second) and thus required use of a tripod. Locale: Lake Superior Provincial Park
Ontario. Lens: Leica 100mm macro. Film: Kodachrome 64.

Notes

When you photograph underwater, everything has to be done with much more deliberation: You ha limited air supply and you can't change film! But the efforts are well worth it: Coral reefs have incredib color and life forms. This is a flamingo tongue cowry grazing on a sea fan. Locale: St. Thomas, U.S. Virg Islands. Camera: Nikonos V. Lens: 35mm Nikkor with closeup attachment. Lighting: Nikonos SB 1 underwater strobe. Film: Kodachrome 64.

Notes

Coral life can rival any terrestrial plants and animals for brilliant color. I found these coral polyps huggi
this blue sponge in a cave in about forty feet of water off St. John in the U.S. Virgin Islands. I had to sho
on my back looking straight up, being careful my air bubbles didn't interfere with the shot. Camer
Nikonos V. Lens: 35mm Nikkor with closeup attachment. Film: Ektachrome 100.

Notes

Aspen. Tall, stately, elegant. I wanted to convey that, so I chose to isolate on a portion of the tree by usi
a telephoto. Framing it as a vertical photograph strengthens the feeling of tallness. And overcast lighti
lends a softness, a quiet mood to the picture. Locale: Colorado's Elk River Valley. Lens: Leica 70-210m
zoom at 200mm. Film: Kodachrome 64.

Notes

Home Ranch in northern Colorado has this wonderful old rowboat on a little trout pond. Visually photographically, it's a delight. Early in the morning, before the sun came up, I photographed composing so that it's in the *center* of the picture (breaking one of the rules of composition). T arrangement conveys a nice sense of tranquility and peacefulness to the scene. Lens: Leica 70-210r zoom. Film: Fujichrome 50.

Notes

This waterfall, high in Colorado's Mt. Zirkel Wilderness Area, is located in a narrow, shaded canyon. Wi
clear, open blue sky above, I knew the rendition would have some blueness to it, but I didn't correct for
with filters because that color conveys a strong sense of the crisp coldness of mountain water. Lens: Lei
70-210mm zoom. Film: Kodachrome 64. Shutter speed: 1/8 second to blur the falling water.

Notes

These columbines, growing near timberline in Wyoming's Snowy Range, have long stalks and wave in th slightest breeze. Under these conditions you've got to have patience. Set up the camera on a tripod, g everything set, and wait until things are still. Overcast light gives a nice softness to the scene. Len Leica 100mm macro. Film: Fujichrome 100.

Notes

One of my favorite plants in the Rocky Mountains is the false hellebore. In spring when its just coming u the leaves unfurl in graceful curves, with wonderful patterns and textures. I utilized soft overcast lig here; bright sunlight would have been too harsh and the delicacy of the textured leaves would have be lost. Lens: Leica 100mm macro. Film: Kodachrome 64.

Notes

There's a mistaken impression that the best landscape photographs are made with a wide-angle lens. fact, just the opposite is often true: The best landscapes are frequently captured with a telephoto len With a telephoto, you can reach out and isolate a significant portion of the scene. And the compress perspective dramatizes background elements like Wyoming's Pilot Peak near Yellowstone National Par A wide angle would have diminished the size of the mountain. Lens: 250mm Sonnar on a Hasselblad. Fil Ektachrome 64.

Notes

I liked the clean simplicity of this scene in Colorado's San Luis Valley: a field, three trees, a line of dista
mountains, the cloud. Placing the horizon line very low in the picture also creates a strong sense
openness and spaciousness. When shooting landscapes, avoid the temptation of cramming too much in
you'll end up with visually cluttered pictures. Keep 'em simple. Lens: 250mm Sonnar on a Hasselbla
Film: Ektachrome 64.

Notes

Cold winter weather takes its toll on electronic cameras with batteries. If the batteries die, so does tl camera. So I chose my trusty, batteryless Hasselblad camera for a ski touring trip in Wyoming's Grai Teton National Park in the middle of winter. It hit twenty below zero, but the Hasselblad kept clicking. F this shot of a clearing storm near sunset, I chose *not* to use a warming filter. Instead, I knew that tl Ektachrome film would give an exaggerated blue to the scene, enhancing the frigid feeling. Lens: 150m Sonnar. Film: Ektachrome 64.

Notes

To capture the feeling of the rushing water of a mountain stream, I used a one-second shutter speed wi
the Hasselblad camera mounted on a tripod. The slow shutter speed allows the water to become a bl
imparting the sense of movement or motion. The locale is Wyoming's Snowy Range. Lens: 250m
Sonnar. Film: Fujichrome 50.

Notes

I was on an assignment for *Conde Nast Traveler* magazine, at a remote lake in British Columbia, a
discovered these incredible fields of Indian paintbrushes. I wanted a tight shot of an individual flower,
the same time conveying a feeling of a whole field of them. I used a Leica 180 lens on an extension tu
shooting wide open. I was actually shooting through some other flowers and the shallow depth of fi
rendered them as a subtle wash of color in the foreground. Film: Fujichrome 100.

Notes

In Canyonlands National Park in Utah, there are fields of a highly unusual plant called stipa grass. I
unusual because it has adapted well to this desert environment. But it's so delicate and ethereal that it
difficult to photograph in a way that has impact. I chose a medium telephoto, a Leica 180mm, and pc
tioned myself so that some of the grasses had a dark background. I used a fairly large aperture
minimum depth of field, so that only a few were sharp, and the rest, unsharp, blended into a mass of col
Film: Kodachrome 64.

Notes

Photography should always be fun. Photograph whatever pleases or tickles you. Don't make a pictu because you think it's what someone else would like. Shoot to please yourself! I often see things th others overlook, like this bright orange glove someone dropped on a deck chair at the Chenik Brown Be Camp in Alaska. What visual incongruity: the muted colors of wood and canvas against the brilliance of t glove. And besides, there's something a little risqué about all this. No way I'm gonna sit in that cha Lens: Leica 70-210mm zoom. Film: Kodachrome 200.

Notes

All afternoon, clouds had been streaming over Chenik Mountain on Kamishak Bay in Alaska. When t
sun slipped behind the mountain at sunset (which is around midnight in June!), it created this blaze of lig
and color. How do you determine exposure for a scene like this? Very carefully. If you let the meter
influenced by the dark mass of mountain, it will overexpose the sky and clouds. I metered from the sk
then bracketed exposures in $^{1}/_{2}$ f-stop increments to fine tune. Lens: Leica 70-210mm zoom. Fil
Kodachrome 200.

Notes

This is the wild Salmon River in the heart of Idaho's River of No Return Wilderness Area. I made this sh on one of my many whitewater raft trips on the Salmon. I wanted to convey a sense of the power o river, and these boulders, tumbled and polished at flood stage, capture that sense. To relate the boulde to the river, I used a 20mm ultra-wide-angle close to the rocks and stopped down to f/22 for maxim depth of field. Film: Kodachrome 64.

Notes

Often the pictures with the strongest impact are those with the simplest composition. These marab storks were perched in an acacia tree in Kenya's Maasai Mara Game Reserve. To isolate on just the tr and birds and sky, I used a long telephoto lens, a Leica 560mm. And I waited until the late afternoon s had sunk lower and gave a golden glow to the landscape. Film: Kodachrome 200.

Notes

Exposure Tips

The metering systems in cameras these days are quite good and are generally reliable. But there are times when meters can be fooled into giving undesirable over- or underexposures. These situations occur when you compose a picture that consists primarily of objects that are very dark or very light. All light meters are based on the assumption that the light reflected from the image is of average brightness, equal to the light that is reflected from a gray card with an 18 percent (also called middle gray) reflectance value, the color of the gray card in the back of this notebook. If you aim your camera at something very light, the meter calls for an exposure to make it middle gray—it underexposes, making the white look gray. Metering a subject with strong backlighting can also cause underexposure of the main subject.

To handle these tricky situations, you can use the gray card (see instructions on how to use it). Or, you can use these helpful tips to gauge the correct exposure:

Sunny 16 Rule: For a bright sunny day, between midmorning and midafternoon, correct exposure can be obtained by using the reciprocal of the ISO film speed as the basic shutter speed (or the closest shutter speed to the reciprocal) and f/16 for aperture. In other words, for ISO 64 film, use 1/60 second for shutter speed at f/16; for ISO 100, use 1/125 at f/16, and so on.

Gray Card Approximations: For some people, the palm of your hand is approximately one f-stop brighter than middle gray: Take a reading from your palm and *open up one f-stop from the meter reading before shooting your subject.* Green grass in summer is close to a middle gray in tonal value. In most low elevations in the northern hemisphere, the northern sky on a cloudless day is close to middle gray. Be careful in higher elevations: The light reflected in the northern sky above 6,000 feet is darker than 18 percent gray.

Add Light to White; Darken the Dark: If you meter a very light or white subject, add light; that is, *open up by at least one f-stop*. When metering from a very dark subject, *stop down about one f-stop*.

In any tricky metering situation, always bracket exposures!

Double and Multiple Exposures

Making two or more exposures on the same frame can be a way of creating visually exciting and interpretive or impressionistic photographs. Elsewhere in this book is a photograph of some flowers; I made the picture by taking sixteen exposures on the same frame, an impressionistic interpretation.

Many cameras have a small lever that allows you to make multiple exposures. If you're not sure, check your camera manual. It's possible to accomplish the same thing by using the film rewind button, but it is a little trickier. You'll need to turn the rewind knob first to take up any film slack, then hold in the rewind button while making exposures. For either method, a motor drive is very useful in making several exposures.

Obviously, some adjustment must be made for the exposure when you start adding one or more images atop another on the same piece of film. Generally, if the subjects being layered on top of one another are of the same tonal value, the exposure should be divided evenly between the individual exposures so as not to overexpose. In other words, in making sixteen exposures on a single frame, each picture should receive one-sixteenth of the correct exposure for one picture—the equivalent of four f-stops.

The easiest way of adjusting exposure is to multiply the ISO film speed by the number of exposures you wish to make and set this on your film speed dial. For example, when you're using ISO 64 film and want to make a double exposure, set the film speed dial to 125 and use the meter in the normal way (and don't forget to reset to normal speed when you're through). Or you can use this chart:

	Film Speed Setting for ISO		
Number of Exposures	**25**	**64**	**100**
2	50	125	200
4	100	250	400
8	200	500	800
16	400	1000	1600
32	800	2000	3200

Results are sometimes hard to visualize, so experiment—and keep notes (that's what this notebook is for!) so you can repeat successes.

Reciprocity Failure in Color Films

This subject sounds a little ominous and intimidating, but it isn't. And it is something you should know about.

In everyday shooting, we can choose among a wide range of f-stop and shutter speed combinations. If the meter indicates a correct exposure of 1/60 second at f/8, we can use 1/8 at f/22, 1/15 at f/16, 1/30 at f/11, 1/125 at f/5.6, 1/250 at f/4, and 1/500 at f/2.8. All will give the proper exposure. However, films lose sensitivity at very short or very long exposures. For practical purposes, we needn't worry about the short end. But long exposures, around one second or longer, may be of concern. If you *don't* make corrections for reciprocity effects, your shots may come out severely underexposed.

In addition to loss of sensitivity, long exposures may cause a color shift—and to give a correct rendition of the subject, you may need to use a color correcting filter. The following chart gives exposure corrections and filter recommendations for a number of commonly used color films.

	Exposure Time (Seconds)		
Film	**1**	**4**	**10**
Kodacolor Gold 100	add 1 stop CC 20Y		NR
Kodacolor Gold 400	add 1/3 stop No filter		add 1 stop No filter
Ektapress Gold 100	add 1 stop CC 20Y		NR
Ektapress Gold 400	add 1/3 stop No filter		add 1 stop No filter
Ektapress Gold 1600	None No filter		add 1 stop No filter
Ektar 25	None No filter		None No filter
Kodachrome 25	add 1/2 stop No filter		NR

Reciprocity Failure in Color Films (continued)

Film	Exposure Time (Seconds) 1	4	10
Kodachrome 64	add 1 stop CC 10R		NR
Kodachrome 200	NR		NR
Ektachrome 64	add 1/2 stop CC 10M		add 1 1/2 stop CC 15M
Ektachrome 100	NR		NR
Ektachrome 100 Plus	add 1/2 stop CC 05R		NR
Ektachrome 200	add 1/2 stop No filter		NR
Ektachrome P800/1600	NR		NR
Fujichrome 50	None No filter	add 1/3 stop CC 05M	add 1/2 stop CC 08M
Fujichrome 100	None No filter	add 1/3 stop CC 05M	add 1/2 stop CC 08M
Fujichrome 400	None No filter	add 1/3 stop CC 02Y	add 1/2 stop CC 02Y

Note: CC indicates color correcting filter: the numbers refer to the density of the filter; Y is yellow, R is red, M is magenta. NR means not recommended.

Cold Weather Photography

Just because the weather turns cold and nasty doesn't mean you have to put the camera away. Winter can be a great time to photograph. Think about those cold, crisp winter mornings when the sun paints the blue landscape with warm colors. Or those little touches of color: a pale autumn leaf trapped in ice or snow; green needles of pines and spruces coated with a white mantle.

A below-freezing temperature can present problems for cameras. Actually, the problem is for camera *batteries*. Modern electronic cameras rely on battery power for everything—light metering, shutters, auto-focusing systems. If the batteries die, so does the camera. Cameras with mechanical shutters and manual focusing still have metering systems that utilize batteries for the light meter. Some precautions:

- Keep the camera zipped inside your parka or coat for warmth.

- When taking the camera out in the cold air, check for any moisture condensation on the lens; if moisture appears, wait for a few moments, then clean it carefully with lens cleaning tissue.

- Carry spare batteries in an inside pocket—pants or shirt—so that they benefit from body warmth.

- When bringing a camera from the cold outdoors to indoors, be careful of moisture condensation: Slip the camera into a plastic bag and twist it closed before entering a warm room. Let the moisture collect on the bag, not the camera.

- In very cold temperatures—below zero—advance the film very slowly. The plastic film base can become brittle in extreme cold and cause breakage or tearing of the film.

- Don't use motor drives in very cold temperatures. The batteries will probably die very quickly anyway, but motor drives put a strain on the whole system in subzero temperatures. Stay with a manual film advance.

Nighttime/Low Light Photography

Don't quit shooting when the sun goes down. However, most light metering systems aren't sensitive enough to give accurate exposures in low light. So the table below gives some approximate exposures for various nighttime lighting situations. For most of these, a tripod may be necessary. Also, many night scenes are illuminated by tungsten lights which have a warmer color balance than daylight. Regular daylight films may render the scene too red or too yellow, so you many want to use a tungsten-balanced color film: Kodak Ektachrome 160 or Fuji's Fujichrome 160 (use the exposure guidelines for ISO 200 and open up one-half f-stop). Remember, these are only rough guidelines to be used as a starting point. Bracket your exposures!

Subject / Film Speed:	ISO 64	ISO 200	ISO 400
Interior of homes (average)	1/4 at f/2.8	1/15 at f/2	1/30 at f/2
Interior of homes (bright)	1/15 at f/2	1/30 at f/2	1/30 at f/2.8
Candlelit subject	1/4 at f/2	1/8 at f/2	1/15 at f/2
Christmas lights and trees (indoors)	1/2 at f/2.8	1/4 at f/2.8	1/4 at f/4
Christmas lights and trees (outdoors, with snow)	1/30 at f/2	1/30 at f/2.8	1/60 at f/2.8
Street scenes (brightly lit)	1/30 at f/2	1/30 at f/2.8	1/60 at f/2.8
Store windows	1/30 at f/2.8	1/30 at f/4	1/60 at f/4
Buildings, monuments, and fountains (floodlight lit)	1/2 at f/2.8	1/4 at f/2.8	1/8 at f/2.8
Skyline (ten minutes after sunset)	1/30 at f/4	1/60 at f/4	1/60 at f/5.6
Skyline (right after sunset)	1/60 at f/4	1/60 at f/5.6	1/60 at f/8
Traffic (moving, with light patterns)	20 sec at f/16	10 sec at f/16	10 sec at f/22
Fairs and amusement parks	1/15 at f/2	1/30 at f/2	1/30 at f/2.8
Campfires	1/30 at f/2.8	1/30 at f/4	1/60 at f/4
Subjects lit by campfires	1/8 at f/2	1/15 at f/2	1/30 at f/2
Football games (floodlight lit)	1/30 at f/2.8	1/60 at f/2.8	1/125 at f/2.8
Moonlit landscapes (moon not in picture)	4 min at f/2.8	2 min at f/2.8	1 min at f/2.8
Moonlit snowscapes (moon not in picture)	2 min at f/2.8	1 min at f/2.8	30 sec at f/2.8
Circuses and stageshows (floodlight lit)	1/30 at f/2	1/60 at f/2	1/60 at f/2.8
Circuses and stageshows (spotlight lit)	1/60 at f/2.8	1/60 at f/4	1/60 at f/5.6
Museums and art galleries (well lit)	1/8 at f/2	1/15 at f/2	1/30 at f/2
Fireworks (shutter open, on B*)	f/8	f/16	f/22
Moon (telephoto closeup)	1/125 at f/8	1/250 at f/8	1/500 at f/8
Lightning (shutter open, on B*)	f/5.6	f/8	f/11

*Note: For fireworks and lightning, set shutter on B and hold it open with a locking cable release. To capture several bursts or lightning strikes, leave the shutter open and block the camera lens between events.

Shooting the Moon

For photographing the full moon, conventional wisdom suggests that since the moon is illuminated by the sun, the "Sunny 16" rule of exposure should apply. In other words, the reciprocal of the film speed at f/16 should give the correct exposure. Unfortunately, it doesn't quite work—the moon comes out too dark. Actually, you should use a "Sunny 11" rule for this one: For ISO 64 film, choose 1/60 second shutter speed at f/11 (or equivalent f/stop-shutter speed combination) for correct exposure. The chart below is based on the "Sunny 11" rule.

The moon will be rendered more dramatic by using a long telephoto lens—400mm, 500mm, or 600mm. Mount the lens on a sturdy tripod and use the fastest shutter speed possible with the lens wide open. For example, using a lens with a maximum aperture of f/5.6 and ISO 64 film, use 1/250 second shutter speed. This will minimize any image blur due to shaking of the camera, lens, and tripod. Finally, bracket your exposures one-half f-stop on either side of the indicated exposure.

The values given in this chart are for crisp, clear nights with no clouds or haze. If there is thin cloud cover or haze, use these values as a starting point and bracket over a wider range of exposures.

Phase	**ISO**	**Exposure**	**ISO**	**Exposure**
Full Moon	64	1/250 at f/5.6	100	1/500 at f/5.6
Half Moon	64	1/60 at f/5.6	100	1/125 at f/5.6
Crescent Moon	64	1/8 at f/5.6	100	1/15 at f/5.6

The above figures apply only to exposures made at least one hour after dark. If you shoot a landscape in which the full moon has just risen above the horizon, use normal metering methods for exposure, but be careful—*don't* meter off dark shadows on the land. It's best to split the exposure between land and sky, with a bit of emphasis on the sky. And bracket exposures.

Names and Addresses

Name____

Address______________________________________

____

Phone_______________________________________

Name____

Address______________________________________

____

Phone_______________________________________

Name____

Address______________________________________

____

Phone_______________________________________

Name____

Address______________________________________

____

Phone_______________________________________

Name____

Address______________________________________

____

Phone_______________________________________

Name____

Address______________________________________

____

Phone_______________________________________

Name____

Address______________________________________

____

Phone_______________________________________

Names and Addresses

Name____

Address______________________________________

____

Phone____

Name____

Address______________________________________

____

Phone____

Name____

Address______________________________________

____

Phone____

Name____

Address______________________________________

____

Phone____

Name____

Address______________________________________

____

Phone____

Name____

Address______________________________________

____

Phone____

Name____

Address______________________________________

____

Phone____

Names and Addresses

ame____

ddress____

____

hone____

ame____

ddress____

____

hone____

ame____

ddress____

____

hone____

ame____

ddress____

____

hone____

ame____

ddress____

____

hone____

ame____

ddress____

____

hone____

Name____

Address____

____

Phone____

Names and Addresses

Name____

Address______________________________________

____

Phone____

Name____

Address______________________________________

____

Phone____

Name____

Address______________________________________

____

Phone____

Name____

Address______________________________________

____

Phone____

Name____

Address______________________________________

____

Phone____

Name____

Address______________________________________

____

Phone____

Name____

Address______________________________________

____

Phone____

Names and Addresses

ame______________________________

ddress______________________________

____

hone______________________________

ame______________________________

ddress______________________________

____

hone______________________________

ame______________________________

ddress______________________________

____

hone______________________________

ame______________________________

ddress______________________________

____

hone______________________________

ame______________________________

ddress______________________________

____

hone______________________________

ame______________________________

ddress______________________________

____

hone______________________________

ame______________________________

ddress______________________________

____

hone______________________________

Photographer's Personal Directory

There are many organizations dedicated to preserving natural areas and wildlife, which is of great benefit to nature photographers. Many animals are endangered by the actions of humans, and it is up to us to see that both animals and the environment receive the protection they need. This is not intended to be an exhaustive list.

African Wildlife Foundation
1717 Massachusetts Avenue NW
Washington, D.C. 20036

Canadian Nature Federation
453 Sussex Drive
Ottawa, Ontairo K1N 6Z4

Canadian Wildlife Federation
1673 Carling Avenue
Ottawa, Ontairo K2A 3Z1

Canadian Wildlife Service
49 Camelot Drive
Nepean, Ontario K1A 0H3

Defenders of Wildlife
1244 Nineteenth Street NW
Washington, D.C. 20036

Ducks Unlimited Canada
1190 Waverly Street
Winnipeg, Manitoba R3T 2E2

Ducks Unlimited
One Waterfowl Way
Long Grove, IL 60047

National Audubon Society
950 Third Avenue
New York, NY 10022

National Wildlife Federation
1412 Sixteenth Street NW
Washington, D.C. 20036

The Nature Conservancy
1800 North Kent Street, Suite 800
Arlington, VA 22209

The Sierra Club
730 Polk Street
San Francisco, CA 94109

Wilderness Society
1400 I Street NW, Tenth Floor
Washington, D.C. 20005

World Wildlife Fund (U.S.)
1250 Twenty-fourth Street NW
Washington, D.C. 20037

For Photographers Who Take Their Work Seriously

Wilderness Photography Workshops with Boyd Norton and Mary Ellen Schultz

For over fifteen years these creative workshops have been conducted in exciting locales across North America and overseas, such as:

Africa (Kenya, Tanzania, Rwanda)
Alaska
Borneo and Bali
California
Colorado
Galápagos Islands
Maine
Ontario
Virgin Islands
Washington
Wyoming

Other instructors with the workshops: Les Line, editor of *Audubon* magazine; Martha Hill, picture editor of *Audubon;* Charles Krebs, nationally known nature photographer.

For information:
Wilderness Photography Workshops
P.O. Box 2605
Evergreen, Colorado 80439 U.S.A.
303-674-3009

More Great Books From Voyageur Press

Photographing Wildflowers
By Craig and Nadine Blacklock. An informative and thorough book that details the basics of closeup photography of wildflowers and the forest floor. The editors of *Outdoor Photographer* aren't the only ones who have been convinced, and they had this to say: ''High quality information. . . lucid and practical insights on everything from subject selection to useful equipment for light control to important tips on what to wear and who to contact for nature photography outings.''

Photographing Waterfowl
By Kit Howard Breen. The author's suggestions begin with the basics and end with sophisticated systems for advanced photography. Breen describes the elements of composition and creativity; color and light; printing, matting, and framing; and includes ideas and references for selling waterfowl photography. *Photographing Waterfowl* covers all the angles.

The Mountain Gorilla
By Boyd Norton. Among the rarest animals on earth, mountain gorillas may number as few as 280 in the wild, and these are concentrated in a shrinking habitat in a rugged region in east central Africa. *The Mountain Gorilla* portrays the land and the life of the mountain gorilla, and explores critical questions about human and gorilla interaction. Illustrated with photography by Boyd Norton.

And look to Voyageur for books about great subjects and great places to photograph:

Apostle Islands
The Arctic Wolf
Black Hills/Badlands: The Web of the West
Boundary Waters Canoe Area Wilderness
The Canada Goose
Everglades
The Geese of Silver Lake
Lake Superior's North Shore and Isle Royale
Love of Loons
Minnesota State Parks
The Sky Islands of Southeast Arizona

Write or call Voyageur Press for a free catalog of over 100 publications.

Voyageur Press
P.O. Box 338, 123 North Second Street
Stillwater, MN 55082 U.S.A.
In Minn 612-430-2210
Toll-free 800-888-9653

wers are such delicate subjects, and they deserve soft lighting to bring out subtle color. Bright sunlight ar too harsh. This shot was made on an overcast day using one of my favorite closeup techniques: a mm lens with extension tube. The shallow depth of field creates nice washes of color for foregrounds for backgrounds. This is a somewhat rare lady's slipper orchid, *Cypripedum guttatum,* found on the stal tundra at Chenik Head, Kamishak Bay, Alaska. Lens: Leica 180mm with extension tube. Film: lachrome 64.

Using the Gray Card

For those times when you are unsure of the exposure to use for a scene or subject, use the gray card. Hold the card so that the light falling on it is from the same angle as that falling on the scene or subject. Focus on the card, filling the frame of the viewfinder as much as possible. Take a reading. If you are using a manually adjustable camera, set the f-stop and shutter speed that gives correct exposure for the gray card reading. If you have an automatic camera, use the exposure lock to hold the reading obtained from the gray card. Then focus on your scene or subject and shoot.

The times when it's important to use a gray card for exposure are when you have a scene or a subject that is very white or bright or one that is very black or dark. Let's say that you have composed a picture of a white swan so that the bird very nearly fills the frame. Your exposure meter is based on an 18 percent gray as an average for proper exposure. If you follow your meter reading, it will give an exposure that will render the bird gray; that is, the swan will be underexposed. To render the bird in its proper white, you will need to open up the aperture one f-stop or more. But if you take your meter reading from the gray card in the same light as the bird, the swan will be rendered correctly and a little more precisely than guessing at how much to open up the aperture.

The opposite situation occurs when you photograph a black cat. The meter measures the reflected light at 18 percent gray—much too light for a black cat. Therefore, the cat will be overexposed and you will need to stop the lens down about one f-stop to render it correctly. Again, using the gray card is more precise.